# WATERMARK

*Clayton T. Michaels*

Cover art by Nancy Botkin

Edited by Dave Bonta and Beth Adams

Book design by ParcMedia.ca

ISBN 978-0-9781749-2-7

First edition printed in the United States
August 2010

*published by*

**qarrtsiluni**

www.qarrtsiluni.com

*in collaboration with*

PHOENICIA PUBLISHING
MONTREAL

www.phoeniciapublishing.com

*We have lingered in the chambers of the sea*
*By sea-girls wreathed with seaweed red and brown*
*Till human voices wake us, and we drown.*

—T.S. Eliot

# Contents

## precious

Bring me sackcloth and oleander.

*Break out the shotguns.*

      *We're going to town.*

Changes in the weather

      tracked on smoke-streaked yellowed windows

      via crosshatches thumbnail-

          scratched into their frames.

Silences breed vacuums small enough

      to hide in the hem of a skirt:

I collect the spent matches as proof.

      (so very precious to no one else but me)

Like the granules of salt I tossed over my left shoulder

and several dozen miles worth

      of broken guitar strings.

There are ashes in the lake.

There are termites in the marrow.

I have aluminum stuck in my teeth.

      (bring me a glass of water and I'll tell you everything)

## icarus

A man with sunstroke is flying
a twin-engine Cessna
over Lake Michigan.

The staler the air in the cockpit grows,
the more positive he is that he sees
St. Peter, walking

across the face of the water,
trolling for perch.
The last coherent thought he has

before being claimed by the water
is of Audrey Hepburn as Holly Golightly,
singing 'Moon River'

on a fire escape. The last thing
he hears the black box
say is *cerulean*.

## the art of sweeping things under the rug

I've been swallowing fistfuls of sand for fear
of floating.

Winter is almost over, and Hell is almost empty…

Look at all the devils, embers
in their eyes.

There is a weight to guilt,

but there is no circumference
to desire.

## fiddler's hearth – summer, 2009

All across the city, the lonely people share a dream about foxes…

We're all drinking Founder's Double Trouble IPA.

The foxes are dancing through a forest, carrying
rice paper umbrellas.

There's a bluegrass band on stage, the fiddle
and mandolin players

trade lead breaks on 'The Black Mountain Rag.'

I'm convinced that I crave salt because I'm dying.

The umbrellas dissolve when they're kissed by the peach
blossom petals

falling around them like summer rain.

The band launches into the Grateful Dead's
'Sugar Magnolia,'

then a long jam on 'Going Down the Road Feeling Bad.'

At one of the sidewalk tables, July sits tapping
her feet and smiling,

skinned knees and larkspur braided into her hair.

## melancholia is a collective noun

There could be hothouses filled with orchids, or a copse
of hard rime-coated trees, or drops
of grey wax in a bowl of water. Or, there could be
nothing after this.

This is the first stage of recovery—
irises the color of wet ashes,
mouth filled with pomegranate seeds
instead of teeth.

At one time we were flowers (at one time, everyone
was flowers), inflorescence on a dogwood tree;
I am an archipelago of splinters, just below the surface,
waiting patiently—

Wrens haunt the cherry trees, clamorously chirping
like Saint Stephen was hiding
underneath, dropping stones and pits
on unwary passers-by.

And Saint Denis, of the lachrymose silences,
carries his head with him for all eternity,
artists never quite agreeing
where his halo should go.

## untitled #19

We never truly fill
the holes—
            we just
learn to live around them,
while the empty
resonates like jade.
Clear and cold.

Strike it right
it almost rings forever.

## hexagram

The Promised Land, apparently, is thick with pines.

Around here, the river smells
like brimstone.

The 24-hour bait shop on the avenue makes its money
selling methamphetamines.

An old dial-tuned radio, set to an AOR station, sits on a shelf
above the crayfish tank.

Through the static, Rick Danko sings about believing in hexagrams.

❋

What shape is the closest synonym for lonely?

Maybe it's the ampersand. One of Klee's dots that went
for a walk and got lost,

preferring vertiginous loops to straight lines—

like Thelonius Monk, wearing a white fur hat and
improvising on 'Epistrophy.'

His piano sounds anxious, an eighth of a beat
out of time,

percussive like the moon when she sashays down
the hallway in a pair

of knee-high black come-fuck-me boots.

❋

I want the moon to be Grace Kelly, the way Hitchcock shot
her first scene in *Rear Window*—

soft focus lens, tight close up on her face,
so that I can pretend

7

I'm Jimmy Stewart gently roused from sleep,

opening my eyes to discover the most beautiful woman
I've ever seen

leaning in to kiss me awake.

## lazarus species

Last night, I dreamt that all my teeth fell
out of my head,

grew back and then fell out again,

while blue copper wires snaked their way
into my veins.

Everyone I know smells like warm milk and lavender.
Everyone I know breeds cancer bats.

These mood swings make me feel ashamed...

Like porcelain, dropped from
a great height

or cinnamon across a windowpane.

## dreaming in dog years

In dog years, I would have died some time
circa 1979.

I'm just following doctor's orders—
brisk daily walks, fish oil

pills for my heart, no sweets
and no liquor—

but the aging yuppies in their cookie-cutter
condos still let

their Jack Russells chase after me.

I'm a virtual ascetic at only
thirty-five,

though I'm not above firebombing
their impatiens

like they were Dresden and this was 1945.

■

I didn't call 9-1-1. I suppose I could have died.

I accidentally set fire to a trashcan in my
parents' garage once—

I had emptied an ashtray before the last cigarette
was completely out.
I used a 25-lb. bag of kitty litter to smother
the larger flames,

then ran glasses of water from the kitchen
until the fire was out.

Oily residue clung to my hair, streaked
my face and hands.

That night I had vivid, adrenaline-jittery
dreams about box elders

that spat mercury-filled helicopter seeds.

The blistered smell of the burnt rubber lingered
in the house for the rest

of the long Fourth of July weekend.

The clocks are all turned back.

In a downtown hospital, my grandfather has
spent three nights

hovering near death—

pneumonic, partial renal failure,
a blood infection.

This morning, the nurses said he was showing
signs of recovery.

He's going to find a way to outlive us all.

I'm thankful for his stubbornness; I hope there's
some of it in me.

I hung up and went for a walk; there was still
frost on the shaded parts

of the condo's lawns, ankle-deep piles of wet,
drifted leaves in the corners

of the subdivision's dead-end streets.

Quiet, except for the scuff of my shoes
on the asphalt

and the music bleeding out of my headphones
into the chilly November air.

## without edges

These are the days that call
for a bottle of Sonoma zinfandel,
that beg for the black pepper,
for the anise. Flavors that at least
warm the mouth. I savor each sip
for as long as I can, until the
astringency makes my tongue
feel like cotton.

Snow again today,
        then rain, then snow.

These are the days I need
a woman without edges, without
unexpected corners that could
tear or scrape. She might taste like
black pepper and anise,
maybe sandalwood incense,
or blackcurrant with a hint of cinnamon.
All flavors to delight in and hold.

We could ride out
the gathering storms in bed,
getting drunk, reading poetry.
              From a distance,
the black type on
the white paper
looks like animal tracks
on the freshly fallen snow.

## anodyne

Summer came late this year. April's
ebony sheets

of rain spilled over into May.

Now hemlock's coming back
in a big way—

hemlock and purple nightshade,

tainting the groundwater, swelling
our tongues

and changing our accents.

Now when I say *trust* it
sounds like *gun*;

when I say *love* it sounds
like *mycosis*.

# chokecherry

I just like the word, really. *chokecherry.*
for a couple of reasons. partly because
it's a fun word to say. the combination

of sounds is almost like a curse word.
only harsher. instead of a soft fricative
like in *fuck*—which is also a fun word

to say—you get the abrasive affricate,
the *ch*, before the hard stop. the *k.* and
then another affricate. it keeps the mouth

busy. to pronounce it properly, you have
to take your time. savor the phonemes.
*chokecherry. choke. cherry.* and I like it

partly because of the image it brings
to mind. a malevolent little berry, brow
furrowed and always scheming, spreading

ill will wherever it happens to flower and
mature. it brings to mind other good words,
like astringent, which brings to mind witch

hazel and red wine. *chokecherry.* doesn't
seem right that it's only toxic to horses,
and that's only after it's started to wilt,

releasing cyanide, making the leaves taste
sweeter. making, as dr. urbino might add,
everything smell like toasted almonds and

unrequited love. *chokecherry.* bitter but
essentially harmless. not like *cheat* or *fake.*
nothing like *fight.* harmless, unlike *kiss.*

## watermark

Right now I feel so goddamn rock-and-roll—
like a grinning

Keith Richards death's-head.

You can see my watermark if you hold me to the light.

The brain needs oxygen. The humors need war
and rumors of war,

and myths about resurrections,

songs about car crashes half remembered
from a fevered dream—

I woke up cleaning gravel from the strawberry
on my knee.

(sing louder now)

## hurricane season

In my dreams you are alive
and you are crying,
half-sick with the thrill that comes
from fracturing your fingers
holding on to fracturing things.

(putting a masking tape X across a windowpane
won't really keep the glass from shattering)

Your disappointments, laid end-to-end,
would stretch from here
to the Atlantic,
the kinder of our oceans,
which only wants the bodies and not the land.

Along every boardwalk, nervous
hotel managers and restaurateurs
pull their aluminum shutters closed.

It's hurricane season.
The sky is a harpsichord canvas;
I am in retrograde.

## tantric

I'm only trying to protect myself—

someone keeps jabbing needles
into my eye.

Spiderweb cracks accentuate the red filaments

and she keeps making these sounds
like the whirr of cicadas.

The whole thing's kind of tantric:

makes me want to bury the bones
of a sparrow

near the bend in the river,

tattoo *f*-shaped sound-holes
over my ribcage,

place a line of salt on every windowsill,
across every doorway,

then melt down the silver
in her tongue

and use it to make rain.

## drylung

This is what the world
will look like

when all the water leaves.

Cracked blue tempera in a yellow styrofoam
egg carton.

Our mouths will fill with gravel

and we will learn to speak
in stones.

## caryatid

It would be different,
        of course—

        if my path were
lined with votive statues. Supplicatory

offerings  buried at their feet:
leather purses filled with coins,

jewel-encrusted amulets,
spearheads. Scraps of papyrus

asking the gods for some
small kindness.

        If I were all
marble and black limestone.

A sanctuary for the artifacts
the people hold most holy:

wooden effigies not carved
by human hands, saltwater wells,

olive trees, burial places of
mythical kings.

        If you were
worthy of enshrinement

in a noble-gas-filled glass
chamber alongside

the rest

        of the caryatids.

## eleemosynary

Speaking of sons, the Psalms say that blessed is the man
whose quiver is full of arrows,

proving that the potential for violence can be
a metaphor for anything.

Bury your sons to their necks in fertile loam, harvest
the flowers from their throats:

stargazer lilies for ambition, magnolia for dignity,
lavender for distrust.

When I was in the loam, an unkindness of ravens
plucked white tulip bulbs

from my throat; forgiveness doesn't
grow here.

A friend once told me that the trouble with men
is their mouths.

I'd like to think she meant that, at least partly,
in a good way—

that a few sleepy, red wine-stained kisses can atone
for almost anything,

and that our tongues are essentially benevolent.
I think Richard Brautigan got it right

at the end of his story 'The Betrayed Kingdom,'
when he wrote:

*people need a little loving and, god, sometimes it's sad all the shit
they have to go through to find some.*

A little kindness: that's all anybody really wants.
Kindness, distractible as crows,

lonely as a frontage road in a non-descript
Midwestern town—

one where the marquee outside the drive-in theater
still reads *closed for the season,*

just like it has since October of '86 and the last Friday
midnight showing

of *Rust Never Sleeps.* And while Neil Young flickered
on the screen,

a young couple in a wood-paneled station wagon
in the back row

inched a little closer, trying to stave off
the creeping autumn chill.

## like a neil young song

Everything sounds sadder in a
reed thin falsetto.
Like a Neil Young song
circa *After the Gold Rush*
1970 or 72.

The words almost cease to
matter when a voice is
spread that thin.
When with one stray syllable
the entire fragile
dynamic can just dissolve.

Then again, sometimes when it
breaks it can be far more
compelling—see
"Mellow My Mind"
from *Tonight's the Night*.

In a reed thin falsetto:
should you ever choose to,
this is how I would like
you to remember me.

## notes

'precious' – the italicized line is from the Norma Jean song 'A Grand Scene from a Color Film'

'the art of sweeping under the rug' takes it's title from an episode of Ingmar Bergman's *Scenes from a Marriage*

'fiddler's hearth – summer, 2009' owes something to Akira Kurosawa's film *Dreams*

'lazarus species' owes something to the band Cancer Bats

'dreaming in dog years' takes its title from a song by The Red Chord

'without edges' takes its title from a song by Superchunk

'hurricane season' owes something to both Olivia Tremor Control and Neutral Milk Hotel

'tantric' owes something to Ani DiFranco and to Takashi Miike's film *Audition*

## acknowledgements

Thanks to the editors of the following journals, where some of these poems, occasionally in slightly different form, first appeared:

*Anti-* : 'icarus,' 'melancholia is a collective noun,' 'watermark'

*Chiron Review* : 'chokecherry'

*>kill author* : 'anodyne,' 'tantric'

*LiteraryMary* : 'without edges'

*Makeout Creek* : 'precious'

*Nerve Cowboy* : 'untitled #19,' 'like a neil young song'

*Oak Bend Review* : 'hurricane season'

*Prism Review* : 'eleemosynary,' 'hexagram'

*Tipton Poetry Journal* : 'fiddler's hearth – summer, 2009'

*Writers' Bloc* : 'caryatid'

Thanks also to NB and DDL for all their help with earlier drafts of many of these poems.

## a note on the award

*Watermark*, by Clayton T. Michaels, was the first-place winner of the 2010 *qarrtsiluni* poetry chapbook contest, selected by Ken Lamberton.

*Watermark* was simultaneously published in electronic form and as a downloadable audio file at watermarkpoems.com, and in this print edition, available through the publisher's website, www.phoeniciapublishing.com, and through Amazon.com.

## about the author

Clayton T. Michaels is a teacher, poet and musician who currently resides in Granger, Indiana. He has been a featured poet at the online journal *Anti-,* and his poems have appeared in *The Prism Review, Nerve Cowboy, >kill author, Makeout Creek, Slipstream,* and *The Chiron Review,* among others. He currently teaches composition, creative writing, and comic book-related courses at Indiana University South Bend. He can be found online at claytonmichaelspoetry.wordpress.com

www.ingramcontent.com/pod-product-compliance
Lightning Source LLC
Chambersburg PA
CBHW071804020426
42331CB00008B/2404